The Forward book of poetry

2011

To Martin Thomas

Contents

HIGHLY COMMENDED POEMS 2010

Preface

Poetry has an uncanny gift for ghost-writing our own lives. More than once while reading this year's selection I've been struck by poems in which ways of experiencing the world feel at once brand new, but also peculiarly familiar. Poets have an enviable knack of capturing thoughts, ideas and experiences that the rest of us are too busy – or if you like, too lazy – to pin down for ourselves. But, of course, this is far from their only skill. It's the putting of those often remarkably subtle and evanescent thoughts, experiences and ideas into memorable speech (to use W H Auden's famous description) that makes a good poem, and one that is, above all, an actual physical pleasure to read out loud; surely still the best test of a poem's immediate and lasting worth.

It's encouraging to report that the standard of entries was as high, this year, as ever, which I think bears testimony to not only the rude health of poetry in this country but also (if you'll forgive a little immodesty) the reputation of the Forward Prizes themselves. I certainly don't envy the hard work that our judges this year have had to do, and the difficult choices they have had to make. My thanks to them: to Ruth Padel, who chaired the panel with such skill, and to her fellow judges, Alex Clark, Dreadlockalien, Fiona Shaw and Hugo Williams.

Supporting them, as always, have been our sponsors: Felix Dennis; Nick McDowell and Arts Council England; Faber and Faber; the Colman Getty team, including Dotti Irving, Liz Sich, Kate Wright-Morris, Sarah Watson and Truda Spruyt; and at Forward, the inimitable team of Will Scott, Lucy Naylor, Casey Jones and Christopher Stocks.

William Sieghart

Foreword

IT HAS BEEN AN AMAZINGLY GOOD YEAR FOR POETRY, with an unusually
wide range as well as an unusually high standard of poem. When the
judges of the 2010 Forward Prizes met to decide the shortlists for the
three categories – Best Collection, Best First Collection and Best Single
Poem – we were carrying enormous bags of books. Boxloads had been
arriving on our doorsteps for weeks. The names of the poets, as well
as the poems themselves, were dazzling. There were international
luminaries, Nobel Prize-winners, well-known and much-loved British
voices, and many exciting newcomers.

We were five readers passionately but differently engaged with
words and how words behave together on the page, in the ear, on stage
and in the mind. Three of us were poets: in addition to myself there
was the T S Eliot Prize-winner and TLS columnist Hugo Williams; and
Richard Grant, otherwise known as Dreadlockalien, a live literature
performer and host of BBC Radio 4's Poetry Slam, who was Birmingham
Poet Laureate 2005-2006. There was also the journalist and broadcaster
Alex Clark and the actress Fiona Shaw, whose spellbinding readings
of T S Eliot's *The Waste Land* were hailed as the perfect meeting of
performance and architecture.

We spent eight hours together, reading poems aloud, going back to
books, to poems again and again, wanting to do the best by them all.
We read beautiful lyrics, brilliant modernists and some very funny
daredevil surrealists. There were a great many prose poems – or perhaps
I should call them passages of prose composed with poetry's kitbox.
Whether this was coincidence or a trend we could not tell, but they are
represented in this book by an extract from Lachlan Mackinnon's 'The
Book of Emma' and Simon Armitage's wonderfully funny 'Poodles'.
There was also – was this another coincidence? – an unusual number
of poems about aunts, represented here by Jo Shapcott's poignant and
imaginative poem 'Somewhat Unravelled'.

It was agonising paring all these books and poems down to three
shortlists. We all had to give up work we loved and admired, which in
other years would have been on the shortlists. Every set of five judges is
different: what we eventually chose represents our particular take on
the brilliant variety of poetry and poetry publishing in Britain today.

It is a brave thing to run a small specialist poetry press, especially in today's economic climate. So we were delighted, at the end, to realise that our shortlist for Best First Collection included books published by several small presses: Peepal Tree, Cinnamon Press, Tall Lighthouse and Shearsman Books, as well as Seren and Cape.

For this anthology we chose two poems from each of the books shortlisted for Best Collection. Seamus Heaney's *Human Chain* is driven by the onset and survival of life-threatening illness. 'Had I not been awake' might speak for all poets: it is about the luck of being 'awake' at the right time, when the right wind, inspiration, idea or poem suddenly comes and whispers in your ear. Lachlan Mackinnon's *Small Hours* is full of poignant elegies and personal portraits. We chose one prose passage from the remarkable series 'The Book of Emma', which occupies the second half of the collection, and a lyric, 'In Memory of Keith Darvill'.

The poems in Sinéad Morrissey's fourth collection, *Through the Square Window*, explore pregnancy and infancy. It is the opposite, however, of cosy: these are expertly calibrated poems haunted by the uncanny. 'The Innocents' conjures the house in Henry James' story *The Turn of the Screw*, and 'Through the Square Window' is a beautifully achieved dream poem about the dead, with a twist about the sleeper at the end.

Robin Robertson's collection *The Wrecking Light* is uncanny and dreamlike in a different way, haunted by a sense of mutilatedness, of deformity under the surface, as in the girl with the hare lip and her 'stone-baby' in 'By Clachan Bridge'. The title theme of Fiona Sampson's book *Rough Music* is the Breughelesque scapegoating, the 'rough music' portrayed in Hardy's *Mayor of Casterbridge* when the townspeople, accompanied by jingly hobbyhorse music, parade effigies of two outed ex-lovers. The adulterous woman, now married to someone else, had thought her secret was safe at last and expires from shock. Betrayal runs through Sampson's book: not by people so much as by reality, both of the world and of language. But betrayal seems to bring the possibility of renewal, too. In 'The Betrayal' something is 'broken' but through the brokenness comes something 'new'.

Jo Shapcott's *Of Mutability*, her first collection for many years, is an astonishing, imaginative reach into the abysses of physicality. The title poem pitches us into the world of our own cells. 'I don't know a soul who doesn't feel small / among the numbers'. As in Seamus Heaney's collection, a life-threatening illness is addressed and survived. By putting this illness obliquely and generously in the wider contexts of space, of 'eclipses, gold leaf, comets, angels, chandeliers', and by the exact lithe way the words react to each other in the line, she reminds us what we need poetry for – to renew ourselves by sharing what new things are beautiful, in the face of mortality and loss.

We have also included two poems each from the books shortlisted for Best First Collection: six very different examples of imagination, humour, sophistication and panache. Christian Campbell is a wildly imaginative, beautifully controlled new Caribbean voice. His poems merge and braid the languages and geographies of New and Old Worlds. Both the language and style of Hilary Menos somehow manage to be tender and sophisticated at the same time; Abegail Morley's unsettling poems are daringly alive; Helen Oswald's poems turn on people, their separations and connections. There is a potent sense of 'we' here, of lives we make together on this 'second-hand planet'. Steve Spence's hilarious pirates get everywhere and won't leave your imagination once you let them in, and Sam Willetts' is an extraordinarily mature first collection. His beautiful poems are haunted by heroin and waste, but the book gradually moves towards detox, recovery, rebirth.

There are also the six shortlisted poems for the prize of Best Single Poem, delightfully varied in their humour, attack, voice and imagination. We have also added our Highly Commended poems from those put forward for Best Single Poem or from other collections. One, Jorie Graham's 'Untitled', unfortunately cannot be reproduced within the formatting of this book. However, you can read this very original work of art at www.lrb.co.uk, the London Review of Books website.

Out of all the Highly Commended poems, I should like to highlight Elaine Feinstein's powerful and poignant poem 'Christmas Day in Willesden Green', written for her autistic grandson. For me, this sums up what poetry does better than any other form; and therefore under-lines the whole point of the Forward Prizes: to demonstrate that today's poets are making art, with true integrity and originality, out of the most painful and central human experiences of our own or any other time.

I'd like to thank my fellow judges, and all the poets whose work we read. There is going to be another agonising round of choosing in

October, when we shall decide the winner in each category. But the biggest winners, I think, are poetry's readers. Prizes are competition, which engenders complicated negative as well as positive feelings. But what matters above all is that people find their attention drawn to poems they would not otherwise encounter, and see their own lives enriched and illuminated by new poems written in our own day, for all of us.

Ruth Padel, *July 2010*

Shortlisted Poems
The Forward Prize for Best Collection

Seamus Heaney

'HAD I NOT BEEN AWAKE'

Had I not been awake I would have missed it,
A wind that rose and whirled until the roof
Pattered with quick leaves off the sycamore

And got me up, the whole of me a-patter,
Alive and ticking like an electric fence:
Had I not been awake I would have missed it,

It came and went so unexpectedly
And almost it seemed dangerously,
Returning like an animal to the house,

A courier blast that there and then
Lapsed ordinary. But not ever
After. And not now.

Miracle

Not the one who takes up his bed and walks
But the ones who have known him all along
And carry him in –

Their shoulders numb, the ache and stoop deeplocked
In their backs, the stretcher handles
Slippery with sweat. And no let-up

Until he's strapped on tight, made tiltable
And raised to the tiled roof, then lowered for healing.
Be mindful of them as they stand and wait

For the burn of the paid-out ropes to cool,
Their slight lightheadedness and incredulity
To pass, those ones who had known him all along.

Lachlan Mackinnon

from THE BOOK OF EMMA

IX

Your girlhood is invisible to me. I find myself rereading your father's obituary. He died this year at eighty-three. His life is on line. He is praised for his work in conservation. He saved the island of Lundy from dereliction. He was an oarsman in his youth. He was born into a banking family and became a banker. He was briefly a Member of Parliament. He was appointed a Lord Lieutenant. He resigned because he found it tedious. A knight and a Companion of Honour. Financier landowner philanthropist. He had two sons and three daughters. I only ever knew of one brother and one sister. One daughter is said to have predeceased him. Predeceased. Like some weird elementary particle you flicker in and out of being. You are given and you are taken away. You are not named. Emma.

In Memory of Keith Darvill
1940-2008

I

I could tell by the shelves of LPs
which house was yours; I didn't need the number
because their thin spines caught spare light
from the street; pale fishbone parallels.

You had said you were damned if at your age
you would become a morphine-addict.
You had a high pain-threshold
like my father.

At times your dark eyes
glittered, a trickster's,
and at times they were hazed
in reverie.

In the tipsy dawns
of the past, you had sometimes wept
at old songs ('Guantanamera'),
making conversation unnecessary.

Cooking, you were all clenched exuberance,
a pinch, a taste, a pinch, a taste
before you'd suddenly swoop the plates
down to your audience with your invariable 'Eat!'

II

Everything's now too late.
In all our arguments
I was poetry, you
were stage and radio

and a true teacher,
furious on behalf
of films I hadn't seen,
music I hadn't heard,

which didn't just mean Bird
but Smetana,
Pete Seeger,
Jewish celebration songs.

Thanks to our ages,
this was the only friendship
of its kind I shall ever make.
A joke along a bar

began it. Oh, the silences
men keep between them
when what they're keeping back
is what would spoil in being said.

Sinéad Morrissey

Through the Square Window

In my dream the dead have arrived
to wash the windows of my house.
There are no blinds to shut them out with.

The clouds above the Lough are stacked
like the clouds are stacked above Delft.
They have the glutted look of clouds over water.

The heads of the dead are huge. I wonder
if it's my son they're after, his
effortless breath, his ribbon of years –

but he sleeps on unregarded in his cot,
inured, it would seem, quite naturally
to the sluicing and battering and paring back of glass

that delivers this shining exterior…
One blue boy holds a rag in his teeth
between panes like a conjuror.

And then, as suddenly as they came, they go.
And there is a horizon
from which only the clouds stare in,

the massed canopies of Hazelbank,
the severed tip of the Strangford Peninsula,
and a density in the room I find it difficult to breathe in

until I wake, flat on my back with a cork
in my mouth, bottle-stoppered, in fact,
like a herbalist's cure for dropsy.

The Innocents

I've seen rooms used in broad daylight
as though they were dark woods –

says Mrs Grose in a quavering voice;
the Governess holds her breath.

Anna has just been in to announce
that the children are washed

and waiting, ensconced
in their billowing cots upstairs,

their trio of candles flickering.
Their window is a window onto death.

In the kitchen, on the servants'
stairs, but mostly in the garden,

where the follies, statues, gazebos
and hedges clipped to the shapes

of birds and arches
stare on unappalled –

a pact is made. A beetle
crawls out of the mouth of a Cupid.

The Governess is right.
Little Flora giggles and plots.

All over the house, like the singeing
of the edges of the world

in autumn or the fraying
of chintz and lace, the roses

are undressing. Master Miles
lies considering his goodnight kiss.

Robin Robertson

TINSEL

Tune to the frequency of the wood and you'll hear
the deer, breathing; a muscle, tensing; the sigh
of a fieldmouse under an owl. Now

listen to yourself – that friction – the push-and-drag,
the double pulse, the drum. You can hear it, clearly.
You can hear the sound of your body, breaking down.

If you're very quiet, you might pick up loss: or rather
the thin noise that losing makes – *perdition*.
If you're absolutely silent

and still, you can hear nothing
but the sound of nothing: this voice
and its wasting, the soul's tinsel. Listen… Listen…

By Clachan Bridge

for Alasdair Roberts

I remember the girl
with the hare-lip
down by Clachan Bridge,
cutting up fish
to see how they worked;
by morning's end her nails
were black red, her hands
all sequined silver.
She unpuzzled rabbits
to a rickle of bones;
dipped into a dormouse
for the pip of its heart.
She'd open everything,
that girl.
They say they found
wax dolls in her wall,
poppets full of human hair,
but I'd say they're wrong.
What's true is
that the blacksmith's son,
the simpleton,
came down here once
and fathomed her.
Claimed she licked him
clean as a whistle.
I remember the tiny stars
of her hands around her belly
as it grew and grew, and how
after a year, nothing came.
How she said it was still there,
inside her, a stone-baby.
And how I saw her wrists
bangled with scars

and those hands flittering
at her throat,
to the plectrum of bone
she'd hung there.
As to what happened
to the blacksmith's boy,
no one knows
and I'll keep my tongue.
Last thing I heard, the starlings
had started
to mimic her crying,
and she'd found how to fly.

Notes

stone-baby: the medical term is *lithopedion*; this occurs when a
foetus dies during an ectopic pregnancy, is too large to be
reabsorbed by the body, and calcifies.

Fiona Sampson

Because he could not live with me
    because he was my life,
the truth that could not come to be
    because I was a wife,

he emptied meaning from the words
    that should have guided me –
I kept the compass, lost the lode
    of how things ought to be

and wandered out among the forms
    that might inform a life,
finding cold comfort in each warmth
    because I was a wife.

The Betrayal

Something is broken –
Milk not rising from the floor
to resume the shape of a jug,
the stone splashed
with creamy stars

Something has broken through
what was clear –
It makes a dark star in glass –
the way distance
draws on the unseen

Broken and new
as a staggered chord,
the next moment
comes racing back
along your glance

Jo Shapcott

Of Mutability

Too many of the best cells in my body
are itching, feeling jagged, turning raw
in this spring chill. It's two thousand and four
and I don't know a soul who doesn't feel small
among the numbers. Razor small.
Look down these days to see your feet
mistrust the pavement and your blood tests
turn the doctor's expression grave.

Look up to catch eclipses, gold leaf, comets,
angels, chandeliers, out of the corner of your eye,
join them if you like, learn astrophysics, or
learn folksong, human sacrifice, mortality,
flying, fishing, sex without touching much.
Don't trouble, though, to head anywhere but the sky.

Auntie stands by the kettle, looking at the kettle
and says, help me, help me, where is the kettle?
I say, little auntie, the curlicues and hopscotch grids
unfurling in your brain have hidden it from you. Let me
make you a cup of tea. She says ah ha! but I do
my crossword, don't I, OK not the difficult one, the one
with the wasname? Cryptic clues. Not that. I say,
auntie, little auntie, we were never cryptic
so let's not start now. I appreciate your straight-on talk,
the built-up toilet seats, the way you wish poetry
were just my hobby, our cruises on the stair lift,
your concern about my weight, the special seat in the bath.
We know where we are. She says, nurse told me I
should furniture-walk around the house, holding on to it.
I say, little auntie you are a plump armchair
in flight, a kitchen table on a difficult hike without boots,
you do the sideboard crawl like no one else, you are a sofa
rumba, you go to sleep like a rug. She says,
I don't like eating. Just as well *you've* got
a good appetite. I say littlest auntie, my very little auntie
(because she is shrinking now, in front of me)
let me cook for you, a meal so wholesome and blimmin'
pungent with garlic you will dance on it and
eat it through your feet. Then she says don't you
ever want to go to market and get lost
in pots, fruit and random fabric? Don't you
want to experiment with rain, hide out in storms,
cover your body with a layer only one raindrop
thick? Don't you want to sell your nail-clippings
online? She says, look at you, with all your language,
you never became the flower your mother
wanted but it's not too late, come with me
and rootle in the earth outside my front window,
set yourself in the special bed, the one only
wasname is allowed to garden and we will practise

opening and closing and we'll follow the sun
with our faces until the cows come home.

Shortlisted Poems
The Felix Dennis Prize for Best First Collection

Christian Campbell

Vertigo

for Gwendolyn Brooks and Kiah

A little girl twirls in the airport,
in the line for New York. She looks
like five and already cocks out her chest.
She is adorned with womanish things,
pink plastic bangles and ruffled socks.
She opens and closes her denim jacket
like wings, as she whirls. She will come
back with more pink things (with which
to twirl). Her lips are pursed big-woman
style (she has the kind of top lip with nerve
enough to curve over the bottom one). She is
the colour of coconut candy. Her face
slopes slightly. Her cheeks are full.
Her eyes wear the seriousness
of sun. She answers to her name
and also to Precious. Her name
might be Precious. She does not fear
her smallness. She likes her Bajan
ways. The spinning is all that counts.
She is already not soft and her forehead
is broad and African. If twirling and
smiling went together, she would give
one wide with dimples and her tongue
between her teeth. Singing goes with
twirling and this requires fierceness.
She knows how to hold on to the beauty
of a thing. She acts this way. You'd want
to say "she is a wailing dervish"
or "she is a rainstorm collecting".
You'd want to say "her hair is sectioned
like the parishes" or "look at Oya's

grandchild." But she is just twirling,
which her singing tells and tells. It is just that.
Her plaits are countless today, full
of bluebird barrettes. All else are staring,
sensible and still. The girl gives a whirl.

LIGHTSKINNED ID

for Neruda, for The South

It so happens my id is red.
Check the clues – my lightskinned
parts: underneath my underwear,
if you pull the skin taut; on the white
hand side and down my wrist
where the veins branch out
like green pipes; my foot-bottom
and almost my eyes up close. It used
to be my whole self, until I was
six for sure. But a brownness
took over. Started swimming
at nine, how sun and chlorine
kissed the night into my skin.
There was no turning back.

But my id is good
and redboned. Like slicing open
a pear for the surprise
of its flesh. Look hard:
there's a murmur of bronze
in my skin. I'm a peanut-butter oreo,
an apple dipped in molasses;
I'm a broad dish of crème brûlée.
O the chiaroscuro of my self.

Still not freed from Freud, I'm fried
on the outside. What a brown on me!
Since the colour beneath my colour
is curried. It wants to come out,
my high yellow id. Always on the verge
of beige. It wants me to Ambi my skin,
to blossom peach all over. My id has such
a need. Here it goes with its libido of gold,

clashing with the ego, my I, a browner negro,
and the superego, who's a radiant absence
of white. He thinks he's in charge.

It makes me act like I'm
better than people, my id. It wants
what it wants. It makes me lick
melted margarine and steal copper
coins from bums. Makes me
bathe in mango juice. Pour sour
milk down my ears and sign
cheques in blood to prove it.
On the forms I fill in
Other and scribble *Yellow*
on the inside in red ink.
I suck the nectar beneath my skin.

My id's pretty niggerish
(for a mulatto). My id is everyone's
Indian uncle. It's taking me
to Hollywood on an undersong
of cream. My id is colourstruck
with itself. My id is El DeBarge.
My id; its job is to keep it light.
How my id misses the eighties.

If only this amber
at heart were enough.

I have to praise it. I have to lull it
with new roses. Run my fingers
along this sallow river
of desire. Stuck in the plantation
kitchen, black ants dying
in an orgy of honey.

Hilary Menos

BERNARD MANNING PLAYS TOTNES CIVIC HALL

When Bernard Manning played Totnes Civic Hall
the whole town came along. Some bought tickets;
some came to picket in a constructive and caring way.
Terence sang a protest song. We thanked him for sharing.

The wiccans wore woad. Ash sold poems on parchment.
Sky from Tantric Turkeys burned calming patchouli,
assertively chanting the mantra "battery farming
fucks with your karma, man". Bootiful, said Bernard.

The staff of Dartington College took front row seats
in an act of guerrilla theatre. Post-modern, ironic,
Bernard didn't know and didn't care; to him they were
just punters, paying full fare, and not in wheelchairs.

He opened with a sure-fire joke about a gay agoraphobic
who came out and went straight back in, provoking
most of the punters at once, especially the womyn
from Diptford Dykes for Psycho-social Wellbeing.

His carefully chosen gags about wellies and sheep
went down like a fat lamb in slurry. The Mayor had a fit
at his mother-in-law routine. High on quinoa and ginseng,
even the hippies joined in as the crowd stormed the stage.

Bernard fled. As his Roller sped off up the High Street
and shrank to the size of a lentil, the townsfolk united
in transcendental glee. Someone (it may have been me)
said, "That's five hundred quid well spent".

Off My Trolley

Pushing my trolley today I have Ingomar the barbarian.
He is my shopping buddy. He strides through the fresh meat section
advising me on barbarian cuisine in the nineteenth century.
He is unimpressed by shrink-wrap and buy-one-get-one-free,
in fact the whole concept of payment is alien; shopping as raid.
I have learned that he likes his meat raw, grilled or fried,
but stews are for *stentl*, a dialect word which doesn't translate
but involves mice, your mother, and a failure to fornicate.

Fourteen years times fifty two weeks I have wrestled this trolley
trying to find a way to make incomes and outcomes tally.
Ingomar says compared to barbarism it's sheer fucking hell,
especially the queues, give him branding or besieging any day.
I find his outlook refreshing, but I know he won't stay.
Besides, next week I've got Elvis, the week after, Galway Kinnell.

Abegail Morley

Cognitive Behaviour Therapy

She snaps her limbs shut,
sits in the chair,
her hands on her knees
extremities wound so tightly
breath might firecracker her body.

She is installation art
a work in progress
defined by her puppetry.
He tells of a new world.
She sees it before her.

He leaves, and her unforgotten past
cuts her edges.
A scissored paper-chain of a woman
extends across the room.

How to Pour Madness into a Teacup

She hangs her tears at the front of the house
cuts the rain in half and puts time
in the hot black kettle. She sits in the kitchen
reading the teacup full of small dark tears;

it's foretold the man in the wood
hovers in the dark rain above the winding path.
The man is talking to her in moons,
she is laughing to hide her tears

and with little time, she secretly
plants the moons in the dark brown bed.
She shivers, thinks the man is watching
as the jokes of the child dance

on the roof of the house. Tidying,
she carefully puts hot rain in the teacup,
sings as she hangs her tears on a string
and watching the dance, thinks herself mad.

Helen Oswald

The Passion

That year it made a change from cowboys and indians,
my brother's hyena yelp as he scalped me again.
Comanche. We knew about the thrill of blood.

Out in the greenhouse, we sawed wooden stakes
recast from former roles piercing the hearts
of vampires, to nail three crosses.

I tore old bed sheets into strips of loincloth,
anointed the feet of a bear with Pears shampoo
and left it overnight in a geranium Gethsemane.

Our reluctant parents watched
at an upstairs window, mortified and yet
unable to wash their hands of it.

Beneath the holly tree that had supplied
a crown of thorns, two gollies, thieves,
awaited Christ, and me and my brother

stretched to an unruly crowd, yelling:
"Crucify him! Crucify him!"
Two small gods making it all happen.

Against the Pane

This light diviner frisks December glass,
shivers with desire for summer nights.

Cold now, wings half shut,
it dies for the hot stroke of July.

If I touch it, a silvery print
might make me think of angels' wings.

No. I turn my back and press hard
into the dark months ahead.

Steve Spence

& THE PIRATES LOOK INTO THE ABYSS

Pirates communicate with each
other by transmitting & receiving
snatches of sound yet they
meddle in the markets at their
peril. Delivery is completely
free with no minimum order value
& our prices are very reasonable.
This operation is a warning to all
those engaged in criminal activity.

When the revolution came, it was
a revolution of the market. It's as
though he dropped anchor in the
middle of the continent simply in
order to write about the sea.
Such bouts of socialising raise
the possibility that this particular
group of seamen are related. All
pirates are on the minimum wage.

There are many reasons for the
loss of pirate schools but it can
surely be put down to a general
decline in cultural sensibility.
Most of his work is dense with
meaning but the corpse looked on
with uncomprehending admiration.
An elegant feeding ballet is set to
the pirate's own music.

It's a Sombre Picture & One that Chills the Blood

No one can honestly predict
what's going to happen during
the next few weeks. Pirates tend
to be creative types, brimming
with ideas & ready to learn
through trial & error. "But I dislike
intoxicating fluids, I prefer the
bitter truth", said Alice, who just
wanted to set all the mad people free.

Will the pirates thrive or crumble
as the global economy crashes
all around us? Alice sat blowing
perfect smoke rings, a skill she
learned aboard the pirate ship.
Nobody knew what changed the
captain's mind but he was a man
of charm, who talked well & fluently,
with imagination & humour.

"Bearded, muscular & prone to
grunting – I think I like the sound
of prehistoric pirates!" Drink was
mostly taken in moderation yet
the whole process seemed so
mysterious that one hardly knew
how to begin thinking about it.
English pirates have a long history
of relishing the rabbit.

Sam Willetts

TRICK

The unexceptional mystery takes place:
around eleven, love turns to matter, Dad

dead. The ward grows and shrinks, early Spring
breaking promises through the glass.

Dad's untoothed mouth gawps, and its last
O holds one darkness; dark of a worked-out

abandoned mine. His absence is brute
absurdity, his hand soft as vellum.

His new state exposes the stark child of him,
and un-sons me. No answers now to a son's

questions, about this, about the sense,
for all his slightness, of a long life's mass

coming to rest, a settling that churns up
grief in a rounding cloud. Dad

dead; end of the opaque trick
that turns our gold to lead.

Two-Up Two-Down

Downstairs, mother and young daughter
kitchen-clattering in bright saris,
the clean youngest son home in his school-rig,
ambience of warm mutton fat
and Bollywood rejoicings from the video.

Upstairs, behind the sacred filthy door,
the two older brothers are snake-basking
in the caramel rays of their all-night sun
with their scales and weapons and clingfilm,
black teeth and void pinhole eyes

always scanning yours for treachery,
without ever quite meeting them.
The frantic ring-tones, regally ignored,
the piles of heartbreak cash. And between
these worlds, always calm, the father

(like a solicitous pimping concierge)
who might have dabbled once
in the old country, who nods and murmurs
'*Come, come*' most graciously
as he waves you on up the sweating stairs.

Shortlisted Poems
The Forward Prize for Best Single Poem

Kate Bingham

ON HIGHGATE HILL

How it rained
when we caught the bus up Highgate Hill
past Whittington's cat and the hospital.
The driver insisted he was full –
twenty wet children, pleading, shrill:
how it rained.

How it snowed
when the bus got stuck on Highgate Hill
and we stood on the pavement in pumps and heels,
children pelted the windows and wheels –
their walk to school a wild white thrill:
how it snowed.

How it shone:
we held our breath down Highgate Hill
through stinking heat. A teenage girl
chucked study-guides across the aisle,
a boy spat on Swiss Army steel
and it shone,

how it shone;
the children kicked their seats until
the driver came roaring up out of his stall.
He bent in the middle. We saw it all.
The engine turned over. Traffic stood still.
How it shone.

Julia Copus

An Easy Passage

Once she is halfway up there, crouched in her bikini
on the porch roof of her family's house, trembling,
she knows that the one thing she must not do is to think
of the narrow windowsill, the sharp
drop of the stairwell; she must keep her mind
on the friend with whom she is half in love
and who is waiting for her on the blond
gravel somewhere beneath her, keep her mind
on her and on the fact of the open window,
the flimsy, hole-punched, aluminium lever
towards which in a moment she will reach
with the length of her whole body, leaning in
to the warm flank of the house. But first she
steadies herself, still crouching, the grains of the asphalt
hot beneath her toes and fingertips,
a square of petrified beach. Her tiny breasts
rest lightly on her thighs. – What can she know
of the way the world admits us less and less
the more we grow? For now both girls seem
lit, as if from within, their hair and the gold stud
earrings in the first one's ears; for now the house exists
only for them, set back as it is from the long, grey
eye of the street, and far away from the mother
who does not trust her daughter with a key,
the workers about their business in the drab
electroplating factory over the road,
far too, most far, from the flush-faced secretary
who, with her head full of the evening class
she plans to take, or the trip of a lifetime, looks up now
from the stirring omens of the astrology column
at a girl – thirteen if she's a day – standing
in next to nothing in the driveway opposite,
one hand flat against her stomach, one

shielding her eyes to gaze up at a pale calf,
a silver anklet and the five neat *shimmering-
oyster*-painted toenails of an outstretched foot
which catch the sunlight briefly like the
flash of armaments before
dropping gracefully into the shade of the house.

Lydia Fulleylove

NIGHT DRIVE

So when the phone call came, saying
    that we should go back tonight, we were barely
surprised, we might have been waiting
    for it all our lives. We took two cars in case
it did not happen that night and one of us
    at least could drive home to sleep and I
followed my father so as not to lose my way
    through the twisting lanes in the dark
but I think it was marked in my head
    and I would not have faltered even
though all the time I was thinking
    of my mother, the bones stretching
her beautiful skin and her left eye almost
    closed, her face as clear as the rear lights
of my father's car or the sign of the inn
    where we'd eaten that morning.
There was nothing to do but to keep on
    driving, the car flowing between the banks
until at last we were crossing the glare
    of the town to the place where my mother
lay dying, though perhaps not tonight,
    we knew that the end might not be tonight.

Chris Jones

SENTENCES

For months on Tuesday afternoons
I'd swing and lock the three gates from staff room

to B wing, then linger, pick my lines of sight
beneath the nets and railings, Victorian light,

before sidling up to Alim on the ones
sweeping hair and skin of prisoners

in little piles; and here was me
bodied with trees, sun, asking 'where's your poetry?'

*

A small, black handgun shut up Alim:
in a dark bar some crack-head shot at him.

Since this kid was an informer
police closed like a forest, flipped Alim's words over,

proffered rooms with thin daylight and deadening walls:
no visits, no shower, no telephone calls

until the arc of their story undercut his.
He almost hit a whisper telling me this.

*

Alim's poems were packs of terriers
that yapped, turned tail and sniffed the air

for scents locked out beyond the fences;
clattered under mattresses,

clawed around cell doors and stairwells
hard on stale and sluggish smells.

His work played landings, was sold for burn
nailed prizes in the competition

which needled lifers writing heart-felt lines –
who was this guy hardly doing time,

who still had latch keys to his name,
could conjure the bleachy taste of rain

swaying on a ladder of his own words,
scaling the whitewashed prison walls?

*

There was that time Alim watched smoke
fray above his head, when he huddled and joked:

'I did not commit *this* crime,' smuggling words
through twilight as men roared

across the wing. Said: 'I miss Louise most
the moment she walks in – rain freckling her coat

and perfume twined around her wrists and throat;
lisping *Alim, no worries, you'll soon be out.*

Even as she bends there in the flesh
I play out how she'll slip the wire and mesh

past screws believing all their dirty knowledge,
dogs that sniff between her legs;

how she'll halt at the bus stop and gulp deep breaths
of sunshine, cry as she lights a cigarette.'

*

I took Alim for a dealer, and asked him straight.
'Yeah, cunning aren't I?' Not a punt in the dark

for a savvy cleaner to be touting goods
to milky-eyed junkies in his neighbourhood.

I thought how flocks of tenners circled each wing.
There were pink official forms I wouldn't fill in

'this lad sells weed, cut scag, twists of crack…'
as most of what I'd learnt wasn't up for grabs

like: 'this "model" con is lying to me again…'
'this pal's stories are what he'd do to women…'

'this man is crow meat beneath the gantry stairs…'
'this big guy beats inmates in his care…'

Alim was a shade against the window's grille,
his hungry fingers rolling loose tobacco,

training his lighter with a nonchalant flick
as if to ask me 'what the fuck

do you know of trade?' He extended
a hand ('mate'), then turned back into the traffic of men.

*

The day Alim asked me to bring a package in
a sleet-wind chased its tail behind the prison.

Louise, he said, would meet me in Forest Fields
(I pictured the snow-trim on her boots and furs,

the cold, pale colour of her eyes,
her slender fingers cradling the merchandise.)

I'd bear the parcel one dead afternoon
for its contents to be thinned and spooned

and wrapped – the stuff blowing out to smoke
to dust lining toilets' clogged-up throats,

or this fine mist over the pool table's baize;
drifts to fleck sick-beds and guards' dark sleeves.

Alim hailed men who ambled from the showers –
towels round midriffs, tight muscles and tattoos –

tasty perhaps with blades in their hands.
If Alim owed some gang his days were contraband.

'I need to call some friends so stay in touch.
Louise wants to meet you very much.'

*

No talk of cargo next time I saw him
what with the muster of thick-skinned policemen,

punters in cheap suits ranged for the Defence.
Alim propped his brush against the fence.

'I want to forget, when this trial collapses,
low-light and locks, shitty pillows and mattresses,

this taste of sweat that sours everything.
No more wind-blown sobs or midnight hymns,

men in the dead hours screaming cold turkey
or small voice that sings *I hate poetry.*'

He backed towards the wing. 'All I'll need,
when I chip it, is a teenth of good weed,

and swirling ice cubes in a noisy bar, Louise
who'll line up vodka, mobile, car keys.'

*

I called a week later to ask if all was well:
a large bloke with a stammer filled the cell.

Alim had talked of a letter but his words were gone
the way of prison yard cherry blossom.

I weighed my chances of catching him in town
ghosted in a shop front, rain-dogged, head down

or grazing past him on the steps to the station:
an arm around her waist, stopping for no-one.

Ian Pindar

Mrs Beltinska in the Bath

Pavel in profile
his eye at the spy-hole
watches Mrs Beltinska in the bath.

Steam from the spy-hole
rises and unravels in the dark
cold apartment at his back,

where a TV with the sound down
shows the River Vltava
bursting its banks.

And as Prague's metro floods
and the Mala Strana floods
and the Waldstein Palace floods

and the National Theatre floods
and the Kampa Modern Art Museum floods,
Mrs Beltinska sinks her treasures in the suds.

The first Czech bible (1488) is drowned
in sewage water, but the warm orange glow
from Mrs Beltinska's bathroom

coming through the spy-hole
gives an odd kind of halo
to Pavel's head seen from behind.

Lee Sands

On a reach of the Thames, late afternoon,
The sun made clear what was in the air:
Flies and seeds, dust and thistledown.
Better to be there, I thought, than anywhere.

That shine on the water shouldn't go to waste.
It was short-lived eternity; I went with it,
Its sky-struck presence, ambling water-paced,
Meant lightlessness wouldn't overtake me yet.

Plenty of others had the same idea as me
To side with a shining and not ending thing,
To measure or be gauged by its authority,
Their kids excited, dogs occasionally jumping in.

They liked that border between wet and dry,
River-herbs, slanted and out-reaching trees
And the way its courses passed them by,
A courier of bits and darks and leftoffs of the breeze.

Of course, light overtook us, as it said it would,
Families receded, not to be caught
In the dark by the river, losing neighbourhood.
Before I went my towpath way, I thought

Of sky and river trying to interlock:
Then, for a moment, my thought couldn't be stopped
Until it reached a western spot, the rock
Down which the first bead of the river dropped.

Highly Commended Poems

2010

Fleur Adcock

Holding the photograph of Mary Ellen,
my great-grandmother the midwife,
to gaze more closely at her face,
I see on my desk behind the frame
another picture, in another frame:
my blonde granddaughter holding her baby.
They are standing in a doorway,
just off to a lecture on *Beowulf.*

Suddenly a rushing of wings
as the generations between accelerate
like a fan of pages riffling over
or like the frames that rattled past
as I swooped into the anaesthetic
for my tonsillectomy, when I was nine.
Face after face, all with our imprint,
humming forwards. We can do anything.

Simon Armitage

They all looked daft but the horse-dog looked
daftest of all. The cute red bridle and swishing
tail, the saddle and stirrups, the groomed mane.
The hair round its feet had been shaved and
fluffed into hooves. Close up, on its hind, there
were vampire bites where the clippers had steered
too close to the skin. Skin that was blotchy and
rude. I leaned over the rail and whispered,
'You're not a horse, you're a dog.' It bared its
canines and growled: 'Shut the fuck up, son. Forty-
five minutes and down come the dirty bombs – is
that what you want? Now offer me one of those
mints and hold it out in the flat of your hand.
Then hop on.' I was six, with a kitten's face and
the heart of a lamb.

THE LIVES OF THE POETS

They rise early, like just after lunchtime.
Their breath on the mirror confirms their existence.
They should rest a while, but today is crunch time

for a rhyme that stands between now and forever,
time to knuckle down to their monkey business.
They sharpen a quill and pause for a breather.

How well they remember those quarantined villagers,
nursing the plague and begging for aid
with pennies dropped into bowls of vinegar,

yet the suffering helps; when things get cosy a
sugary residue coats the tongue,
hence the grinding of peppercorns into Ambrosia.

Late afternoon, and for meaning or moral
they stand at the window and gaze towards yonder,
at the forked oak or a bird in the laurel,

but their compound eyes play tricks by the hundred:
in the clenched fist they notice the rosebud,
in the pretty rose they see Joe Bugner.

They have pinned their hopes on the incidental:
the plums in the fridge are there for the taking,
as is a snow crystal. They offer so little,

expect even less. A plaque on their houses
is ample reward for the years of fiddling,
for the ink stains on their big girls' blouses,

for shuffling, scratching, occasionally traipsing
up to the post box, for walking behind us
and pulling faces. Mimicking. Aping.

Alison Brackenbury

The Jobbing Welder

He was the biker you employed
Ex-Navy, who stormed down the road
With chrome, blue steel, all uninsured,
When work came, always missing.

Each girlfriend ended with a crash.
Her flat, the compensation cash
Lasted six months, but when at last
The child came, he went missing.

There was the quick black hole of drink,
New barmaids' faces, rings' changed glint.
I wear his boiler suits. I think
Half of each zip was missing.

He left, in debt, botched racing cars,
Bought a Ferrari. In whose bar
Did someone brush him, with fierce eyes,
Each shred of kindness missing?

He pawned his rings. The house was gone.
He flew to Venice, glimpsed his son.
Another boy hacked him from the beam
After he went missing.

His friends poured Stella on his grave.
From the workbench, as though he lived,
Tools disappear. All that you need,
All that you love, goes missing.

Siobhán Campbell

he said it was where folks gave up
grouse shooting and pheasant hunting for Lent,
where boys tongued it home with blackened mouths
after sucking the leaves of the aniseed bush
in the church grounds,
where once, at the dock dance, his sister
made him get back on the ferry without looking round
in case he would see his dead ringer.

She had given him, but not him, a jitterbug earlier,
her fright at the southern accent you could cut
and the look in his gamey eye.
She told Dad that he was the better looking, and she lied.
Still, it was best for the girls of two nations
that neither of them died.

Kwame Dawes

REGENERATION

After his wife, the one who mothered
each dropped seed sprouting wild
on the hillsides, then fathered
those that came, eyes opened wide

and wailing from her vagina;
after she bore the shame of his
mannish disregard – a reminder
that in this island man's bliss

is a patient woman's pain;
after she could take no more
and died dumbly in the rose garden,
he buried her then closed the door

to all women, his unspent seed
spilling out in dreams until that, too,
dried up. Now a dead forgotten need
has awakened in him, all torn and new.

Tom Duddy

The Touch

If a child fell from a tree, or raved
with fever, or a father came in hurt
from the fields, I was the one who raced
down the roads to the far side of the town,
to the house by the river, glad
of the chance to pass one more time
through the high clanking gates
into the avenue that would slow me

to a crunching walk under a dark
cher-cherking, rook-swaying canopy.
It never took more than the one
rat-a-tat-tat to bring to the door
the doctor's wife whose briskly gentle hands
once fixed my collar as I stood in the rain.

Carol Ann Duffy

A RARE BEE

I heard tell of a tale of a rare bee,
kept in a hive in the soul of a wood
by a hermit – hairshirt, heart long hurt –
and that this bee made honey so pure,
when pressed to the pout of a poet
it made her profound; or if smeared
on the smile of a singer it sweetened his sound;
or when eased on the eyes of an artist,
Pablo Picasso lived and breathed;
                              so I saddled my steed.

No birds sang in the branches over my head,
though I saw the wreaths of empty nests
on the ground as I rode – girl, poet, knight –
darker into the trees, where the white hart
was less than a ghost or a thought, was as light
as the written word; legend. But what wasn't going, gone,
I mused, from the land, or the sky, or the sea?
I dismounted my bony horse to walk;
                              out of the silence,
I fancied I heard the bronze buzz of a bee.

So I came to kneel at the hermit's hive –
a little church, a tiny mosque – in a mute glade
where the loner muttered and prayed, blind
as the sun, and saw with my own eyes
one bee dance alone on the air.
I uttered my prayer: *Give me your honey,*
bless my tongue with rhyme, poetry, song.
It flew at my mouth and stung.
Then the terrible tune of the hermit's grief.
Then a gesturing, dying bee
                              on the bier of a leaf.

Elaine Feinstein

for my autistic grandchild

At fourteen, his eyes are dark as wood resin,
his hair red-gold; he is an elf-child
with delicate lips, and pale, unblemished skin.
The scented candles and the roasted goose
with apples in its throat don't interest him.
He flicks a dangled string and sets it loose

snatches a cracker biscuit, shaking off
the smoked fish, and then smiles suddenly
as if amused by some mischievous thought
growing out of a landscape I can't reach,
the unknown pathways lying under speech.
On these cold Christmas windows, heavy rain

begins, like the crackle of crumpled cellophane,
or an untuned radio; while Johnny remains soundless,
like a small bird gathering twigs and loam,
completely absorbed in his own business:
gold wrapping paper and coloured ribbons
are the treasures he brings to his sofa home.

It is the first year in seven the whole family
has eaten with him; we have feared his wild
behaviour and forgotten his misfortune,
as if that pain belonged to other people. Now he is mild,
we relax in noise and wine. Is he bewildered
among so many strangers, or reconciled?

Alistair Findlay

Dancing With Big Eunice

Falkirk Burgh Social Work, 1973-5

Dancing with Big Eunice was,
I must confess,
a complete, knee-trembling experience.

She was a big girl, big and bonnie,
big in tights, and without oany.
She had a bum that come straight doon

from her hips and curved roond
like welded sheets of metal on the bow-sprits
of the *Queen Mary* – she was hairy –

where she needed to be – oan her heid! –
she had ringlets and curls, swirls and swurls,
and her eyes seemed to follow your crotch,

and wink Hi! as you walked by her room.
Her own walk was indescribable but went
something like – *Boom-Boom!*

During the day she typed up court reports,
made tea for perverts, and bad jokes,
and smiled at persons who fancied sheep

or wasted the time of the Bog Road police.
Eunice never wasted anybody's time.
She painted her eyes blue. Her lips

were red and redder grew, the more you
looked and the more she looked at you,
till they became like a great big pouting

nipple, or a marble, anyway, something
round and proud that you'd like to chew,
or maybe you'd like to chew you.

She had power over men, I ken, because
they told me. You know that picture
by Beryl Cook, *Ladies Night*, wi' yon

male stripper stretching oot his g-string
for these big dames to take a look?
Well, Eunice would just have reached

right in and grabbed it saying – Look!
Some'dy's broke the wee thing's neck!
O, she had a tongue, make no mistake,

and I'll tell you this, she used it for
mouth-to-mouth no hesitate, that's what
Eunice called   *a kiss!*

Her lips were soft, her breath was sweet,
you were in her grip, as her tongue unfurled
inside your cheek, and downward drove
towards your feet – where it turned and
growled, then upward hurled until it curled
around your waist, looking – no, licking –
for a label, then *Bang!* it started up and
whanged your y-fronts into double-spin,
no half-loads, no low-heat economic
settings here, just the steady beat of a
heavy-duty rinse, a throbbing pre-wash
tumble, and a superb blow-dry, a non-fast
coloured whirring, a chugg, a sough, that
sucked you up and hung you inside-out
to die, o my o my – nobody ever kissed you
better – except, perhaps, Wee Marion –
though she'll deny it to this day.

John Fuller

THREE TIMES

Three times, like wishes or a warning,
It passed him by and made him cry.
First in the morning.

It came to him like sight unseeing,
That closed a door but drew the light
Into his being.

At seven, is a boy to think
Visions will vanish if you stare
Or if you blink?

It passed into him like the shade
Of someone loved he would betray
Or had betrayed.

Nothing was there where it had been,
No chill, no space, nothing precise
That he had seen.

And then at noon, like unfelt touch
That has a power to thrill, though doing
Nothing much.

At thirty, should a man unclasp
A hand he once imagined taking
In his own grasp?

It passed into him like the ghost
Of someone who'd be lost to him
He loved the most.

The shadows lengthen on the court.
The ball was long, the ball was out.
The ball was short.

And now at evening unheard sound
Entered the busy dreaming head
That it had found.

At seventy a man will hear
An echo of all nothings struck
By his own fear.

It passed into him like a bell
That rang for all his losses, and
For him as well.

What were these apparitions but
A trick of the senses to open doors
That they had shut?

Our grief is inward and compelling.
It's ours, and is our fault.
It needs no telling.

Damian Furniss

THE DUCHESS OF KALIGHAT

The 'Duchess' is a deranged butterfly:
his hair oiled and preened into an unwieldy bun
decorated with jasmine flowers. All the colours
of earth and sky are sewn into his sari,
his face a bloodied powder puff, as he flits
from car to car, rubbing his bodice-busting body
provocatively on the hot bonnets of Marutis
or pressing vermilion lips against the windscreens
of Ambassadors, his throaty voice hooting louder
than all the baying horns around him.

He is the star of every traffic jam:
crooning like Marlene Dietrich, a pouting crone,
handbag swinging like a mace; no one gets in his way.
One shake of his padded hips, his plumped out breasts
and the drivers forgive. He is of the third sex;
his maleness was bound by a cord and cut,
left to bleed dry then poulticed by the sisterhood,
dressed, anointed and scented with musks.

Barely a child, he was never a man,
became her, deserted father and mother
to make a living dancing and singing
new babies into the world – a good purse
or be cursed, end up with another changeling daughter.

At other times she trawls the bazaar
threatening to show off what is missing,
what has been gained, available to real men
at a realistic price. Queen of all vice,
she blesses the streets with gaiety,
sleeps in her own bed – velvet and lace,
silk draped; all things feminine.

But when the ambulance passes her way
she shrieks, stubs her long-holdered cigarette,
and, bowing, waves it by. The sisters inside
are saried in white homespun, blue bordered.
She calls them 'the moths' but they tend
even her kind. She offers them his respect.

Rebecca Goss

Mrs Quigley and I

We bumped into each other
in a department store,
were screwing in her car an hour later.
Continued to do so for weeks, months,
every delicious opportunity we could get.

But yesterday was strange.
She came to me, the morning's rain still caught
in the waxy creases of her coat,
little glass bubbles I wanted to reach out and collect.

She'd found Mr Quigley in the hall,
manic, seething, rattling a dice in its shaker.
He let it roll across the floor, it almost touched her shoes.
'1, 2 or 3, you stay, 4, 5 or 6, you go. Shout out the number!'
He rolled a dice for me, can you believe that?

I loved Mrs Quigley's body,
her breasts, lips, legs. And I liked it married.
Liked covering her with my fingerprints,
so he could wipe them away with his own.

Did you hear that? He rolled a dice for me!
She dropped her shaking head,
the hair dark and damp at her neck.
I touched it lightly, lowered my voice to a lover's whisper,
tell me the number, I said.

Philip Gross

THE PRESENCE
(Barbara Hepworth, Single Form)

A one. A standing
      on its own plinth. Slim
            slicked naked singularity.
What's with it? All
      the presence it contains,
            silt swirling to the surface,
stops there, while light
      taps, taps from the outside
            and is not admitted. That
assurance, that's what makes me
      want to rattle it – me
            like a Visigoth, all gawp
and grievance, at the sack
      of Rome, left staring
            at boneyards of stone and
(that's what winds us up
      into a rage of looting) and
            where did it go? The presence.
Stepped calmly aside
      like one of the gods they
            only half believe in, smug
as a joke they don't want us
      to get. Well, we
            don't   get   it
and won't, till one sunset smoky
      from the burning towns behind us
            I tether my horse to a stone
and lie back with the sky.
      And the boulder leans in
            at the edge of my sleep
and quite suddenly Oh I
      get it. Always had it, but
            to find it, had to come this weary way.

David Harsent

BLOOD

Blood Heat

Full length under a wide white sky in a place like this, or a place
you think you remember, or wherever it is she happens to turn
   her face

to the sun, eyes open a moment, then the flare and crush
of red behind the lids and you at her side to watch the sudden blush

that prickles her skin, the first fine hint of burn, as you get
the tip of your tongue to her cheek for the salt-lick of her sweat.

Blood Relative

His footsteps in yours, the moment of waking that same
redeye view of the world, his dottle deep

in your lung, his kiss your gift to give: the sudden sharp
dip of his head, the bloodbead on a lover's lip,

his arrival in the room your moment of fame,
his easy laugh, his clever guess, his word to the wise the sum

of all you are, all you could ever be, and your other name,
given in passion, in trust, is nothing more than a slip

of the tongue, and no-one but yourself to blame
for the hand-in-hand, the cheek-to-cheek, the side-by-side as
   you sleep.

Bloodstain

Drench of the death-bed that drains to the floorboards and hangs
like a sweat of dew on the ceiling below... and where you found

that graceless image is for you alone to know, but it brings
with it a tang of salt, and a dry day by the sea then comes to mind:

raw sky and a cutting wind that left the man half-blind
from a scrap of something blown in from the other shore,

the tear of blood he caught up with his tongue, the nip of fear
you felt as he put his head in your hands while you took

the mote on the tip of your finger, his shudder-sigh, his empty look
no different now to then, perhaps, except for the dew of the sea
    on his cheek.

Blood Alley

Your childhood token, a sickle of red in the glass, albino eye,
eye of the night-lamped hare; a perfect lob would break the circle...

Now hold it close to the light and every fibril
seems to shred, as heart-blood hangs in water, that same dark dye,

shade of the dress she wore when you had your first full taste
of the pulp of her lip and the spittle off her tongue, the cost

to you being more than you had to give, which is why
the circle must break again and the dream unpick and the child
    be lost.

Bloodvein

(i.m.)

Soft on a leaf, last of the garden exotica, found only at dusk and pale
as the face in the sick-bed except for that long line
going wing-tip to wing-tip, heartstring, nerve-track, a thread you
    might pull

were it not for the way she turns and settles her head, the long vein
in her throat showing lilac by lamplight... The shadows that peel
from her fingers as they spread must be part of some long scene

of doubt and decay where all of this plays out: the fractured pearl
of the creature's eye, the journey from leaf to lamp that has
    long been
written in, like your word to her, like hers to you as she palms the
    bitter pill.

Notes

Blood Alley: The name given to a large marble – a tolley – clear
glass except for a twist of red at its heart.

Bloodvein: The moth of this name is a pale cream colour save for
a line of red that goes from wing-tip to wing-tip.

Rachael Hegarty

COCKLE PICKER

6.2.2004 Morecambe Bay

The waters are rising my love,
soon the waves will lap brittle
cold around my ankles.

Night is making its way
across a cloud stirring sky.
The moon is hidden from us.

We have abandoned our buckets,
full to the brim with cockle shells.
The sea reclaims all its creatures.

You must not worry. We have eaten.
Gua Bin and I are tethered together by rope.
I will not die hungry or alone.

With a stick, I score out a note in the sand.
I know others won't read my letter and
the tide will wash this message away.

Yet I believe word will reach you.
I close my eyes and see you,
straightening up from the vegetable patch,

our infant daughter swaddled on your back.
You are preparing for the typhoon season.
A warm wind blows soft on your face.

You are there and night is here.
Water surrounds us, claims us.
I will be with you, in Fujian, soon.

Tony Hoagland

In Praise of Their Divorce

And when I heard about the divorce of my friends,
I couldn't help but be proud of them,

that man and that woman setting off in different directions,
like pilgrims in a proverb

– him to buy his very own toaster oven,
her seeking a prescription for sleeping pills.

Let us keep in mind the hidden forces
which had struggled underground for years

to push their way to the surface – and that finally did,
cracking the crust, moving the plates of earth apart,

releasing the pent-up energy required
for them to rent their own apartments,

for her to join the softball league for single mothers
for him to read *George the Giraffe* over his speakerphone

at bedtime to the six-year-old.

The bible says, *Be fruitful and multiply*

but is it not also fruitful to subtract and to divide?
Because if marriage is a kind of womb,

divorce is the being born again;
alimony is the placenta one of them will eat;

loneliness is the name of the wet-nurse;
regret is the elementary school;

endurance is the graduation.
So do not say that they are splattered like dropped lasagna

or dead in the head-on collision of clichés
or nailed on the cross of their competing narratives.

What is taken apart is not utterly demolished.
It is like a great mysterious egg in Kansas

that has cracked and hatched two big bewildered birds.
It is two spaceships coming out of retirement,

flying away from their dead world,
the burning booster rocket of divorce
                              falling off behind them,

the bystanders pointing at the sky and saying, *Look*.

Anthony Howell

STRETCH

Three years it's been now since I felt the rain.
We get to shower every now and then.
For storms I'll have to wait as long again.

There is our daily amble round the yard,
But if it's raining – whether soft or hard –
We're banged up by some hydrophobic guard.

When clouds deface a postage stamp of stars,
And drizzle dulls the hum of distant cars,
Try catching drops by reaching through the bars.

To get well soaked would suit me to the ground:
To stand there as the rain fell all around:
To piss in it and revel in the sound.

Tell you one thing, when I'm on the out,
With underwater hands, I'll tickle trout
And sleep rough till I've made up for this drought.

Ishion Hutchinson

REQUIEM FOR AUNT MAY

I

A calm sign in the trees of May: she's dead,
not like this dirge staining the air, her name
recited in the camphor-house where the chalk
figurine, that haberdashery sphinx reclines,
riddled by the TV. There no one faces the calendar,
river-stone talks go under the bridge of condolences,
and land on the old sofa's shoulder. I, her water-child,
keep watch over her laminated Saviour, nailed
into the wall, flipping a coin whose head promises
Daedalus. Someone pries open an album, the cocoon
postcards wail on the line, pronouncing, *Aunt May* –

baker, builder of the yellow stone house, your children
hatched wings while your face was bent in the oven.
The mixing bowls, the wooden spoons, the plastic
bride & groom, knew before the phone alarmed
the night your passing. So you passed, in a floral dress,
a shawl softly tied to your head, the house spring-cleaned.

II

Enters Daedalus, father, dressed in white, hands
in pockets, strolling through prayers and smoke
of the mourning wake. I listen: his limbs
are pure starch. On the veranda, eyeing
the gong-tormented sea, seaweeds streak
his beard, salt rimmed his apologies. I hesitate
at the labyrinth of father and son, red hurt
throbbing my ears from my fall on the poppy grounds,
fog swallowing all that was carried over
years of saying nothing. Silence, this flame

held back before erupting, as an oven after heat
has been sucked from it. I begin in silence
my life, then and there, as a ghost.

Jackie Kay

BLACK RIVER

For Matthew

We took a boat down the Black River,
The water darker than the darkest mirror,
The mangrove roots trailing the river bed –
As if searching for the dead down there.

We passed a tree shocked by the hurricane
Whose spindly limbs had transformed
Into a Rastafarian's dreadlocks
Rising from the river bed's rocks.

We passed crocodiles masquerading as logs
Under the mangroves, and snow egrets
Fluttering like blossom in the branches,
And the river carried us as if carrying us home –

Wherever we were, wherever we came from:
A black river running through our arteries,
A black river putting our hearts at ease,
A black river touching our skin like a lover,

A black river to remind us of our ancestors,
Running through the swamps and secret marshes
When freedom was a belief the river rushes
Passed along the dark water like a breeze.

Then, later, when the river ran to meet the sea,
And the colours changed – black, to brown-black,
    to bright blue –
There was my son at the helm of the boat,
As the boat lifted and crashed and smashed on the
    waves,

And there were the jack fish leaping,
The dolphins' diasporic dive, and those strange birds
– whose name I have forgotten –
Carrying an old song home.

Judy Kendall

WA, HARMONY

The bell goes and I dismiss my class.
Tired and dishevelled, I start to pack away
my papers, wipe off chalk dust,
pack up the tape-deck when, *Teacher, sensei,*

a student hovers, polite, gentle, in need,
at an unobtrusive distance, offering me
a tremulous virgin face while he proceeds
in my hard language to mouth his soft apology

for missing last week's session
because he was unfortunately obliged
(oh teacher, hear out my confession)
to attend the funeral of his grandfather.

His English, slow and careful, broken,
he places in pieces on my gathered notes,
equidistant, partly as if in token
of his loss, partly in the hope

that I will read the spaces in between
the words of me and him, his duty
to the class, his unannounced departure, and fill in
the sadnesses to make consoling harmony,

but, sensing my tiredness and my need to get away
from school at this the end of a long day
and feeling shy, he leaves, and leaves me asking why
in my land we don't make young men this way.

in rain so heavy
with falling blossom, wishing
for you

Gwyneth Lewis

from A HOSPITAL ODYSSEY - BOOK 11

'Wilson, I'm frightened.' A daunting wall
surrounded the garden, it seemed, on all sides,
barbed wire on its apex, impossible to scale.
'Ask for a door to take you inside,'
the dog suggested. So, in her mind's eye

Maris imagined a simple arch.
The three of them entered, only to find
not lush and well-tended gardens but a parched
vista – disordered, abandoned ground.
You could see that it had once been grand:

the eye was drawn by formal flower beds
laid out in complex boxed parterres.
Gazebos and pergolas had led
the attention to a central water feature.
All this was more than half obscured

by scrub and brambles. Japanese knotweed
smothered the outlines, sending astray
all design as it went to seed.
'Don't tell me we've had to come all this way
for this,' said Maris, in dismay.

Ludlow said, 'This is Hardy's body,
his lymphatic system.' 'It's a total mess.'
Maris touched a choked-up gully.
It was full of rotting, tarry foulness
that stank with rankness as it deliquesced

to black ooze running thick and sticky.
'No wonder he's ill, if he has this crud
in his system. I think it's up to me

to clear this jungle and restore his blood.'
And Maris tackled the ground where she stood,

tearing up handfuls of vegetation,
taking her vengeance out on ground elder
and couch grass that grew in such profusion
it robbed all else of earth and air.
The weeds grew back like Hardy's tumour.

She started again, picking up litter –
crisp packets, condoms, bits of plastic dolls,
half-rotted newsprint. 'I must work harder,'
she told herself but thick twitch cables
cut her hands. The earth was marbled

with roots, like fat through meat.
The couch revived – the very soil
was riddled with the parasite.
It rose as fast as Maris pulled
it out. She thought, 'These stubborn tendrils

are stronger than I am.' One single tear
fell to earth, its tiny weight
bending a leaf of maidenhair
which added liquid, to create
the start of a mercury rivulet.

Derek Mahon

ROMANCE

after Rimbaud

1

Nothing is serious when you're seventeen.
One evening, sick of the beer and the lemonade,
the noise and bright lights of the café scene,
you sit out under trees on the promenade.

A scent of lime there in the hot June nights.
The air engulfs you with its summery glow;
not far away the wine fumes and the shouts
float up on a soft breeze from down below.

2

You try to fix your gaze on a patch of blue
framed like a picture in the branchy night
pierced by a star, sharp but dissolving now,
quivering slightly, tiny, perfectly white.

A June night! Seventeen! You're getting drunk.
You sip champagne, the stuff goes to your head;
you wander off, imagining some punk
groupie clinging to you or in your bed.

3

The daft heart drifts to popular romance –
when, suddenly, that nice Charmaine goes by,
delightful in the pale glare of the lamps
under her stuffy father's furious eye.

Since you look interesting, if a little weird,
she throws you an alert and lively glance,
two shoes tickety-boo in the boulevard,
and a soppy song dies on your lips at once.

4

Now you're in love (she giggles at your poem) –
in love, until the holidays are through.
Your pals avoid you, love being 'bad form',
and the next day she grants a rendezvous…!

That evening, back to the rowdy café scene,
ordering up the beer and the lemonade.
Nothing is serious when you're seventeen
and lime trees are in leaf on the promenade.

Tom Mathews

JUST WILLIAMS

This is just to say
That I have left William Carlos William's poems
In the ice box.
Forgive me.
They were so sweet.
But so cold.

Thomas McCarthy

Dave Brubeck at *M on the Bund*, Shanghai

A cloud of sunlit forsythia crashes against glass

This idle and unprepared Palm Sunday:
Quintet brushes of gold, frantic as Dave Brubeck,
Sidle across the window.

The cool cats move closer, waiting for the sun to dance
As it does each Easter. The dust of spring
Makes all of Shanghai sneeze, hurtling mixer and crushed

Ice closer and closer. Give the singer a kiss,
The forsythia says, aggressive with yellow.
Not too far away, but beyond the crowded terrace,

A reception is prepared for the crown of the year.
The sun will be king, messiah and Central Committee,
Ascendant in the sky as each hour goes by;

The hour that expands to hold us, the egg
Of a Chinese Easter beneath our yellowy blossoms.
It is the river Jordan stays far away; it is the song,

Flamingo, and all the other promises
That enter this glamorous bar covered with palm leaves,
Or words carried on a tray of cocktails: *I Never Know.*

Patrick McGuinness

House Clearance

Turn the key: note how the emptiness accumulates
as you come in; how by being here at all you seem to add to it,

until it fills the corridor with that fermented stasis
you both disturb and add to as you move. Pass

through a second door, a portal of stirred air,
ignore the rooms to left and right and take the stairs,

your shoes dislodging dust that billows
up in tiny detonations. You're walking underwater,

the silt explodes beneath your feet; at first you think you'll drown
but what's flashing through your mind in one

slow-motion scattering of greys is not your own life but theirs.
No matter that you still can't breathe – that's how it's always

been in here: even the nothingness is thick as blotting paper
on which their shapes have spread like ink – must, damp,

the outline of a body sketched in mothballs and almost –
memory. The furniture is ghostly beneath the sheets

but the missing pictures are still there, outlined
in frames of dirt on squares of wall now white as bone

surprised beneath the skin. You were in every one of them.
Now you're the last flame in the grate:
Hamlet in his theatre of shadows, their embers at your feet.

W S Merwin

Both of us understood
what a privilege it was
to be out for a walk
with each other
we could tell from our different
heights that this
kind of thing happened
so rarely that it might
not come round again
for me to be allowed
even before I
had started school
to go out for a walk
with Miss Giles
who had just retired
from being a teacher all her life

she was beautiful
in her camel hair coat
that seemed like the autumn leaves
our walk was her idea
we liked listening to each other
her voice was soft and sure
and we went our favorite way
the first time just in case
it was the only time
even though it might be too far
we went all the way
up the Palisades to the place
we called the pinnacle
with its park at the cliff's edge

overlooking the river
it was already a secret
the pinnacle
as we were walking back
when the time was later
than we had realized
and in fact no one
seemed to know where we had been
even when she told them
no one had heard of the pinnacle

and then where did she go

Eiléan Ní Chuilleanáin

BALLINASCARTHY

Is marach an dream úd Caithness dob' ag Gaeil a bhí an lá
                                    – Pádraig Óg Ó Scolaidhe

There, where the bard Ó Scolaidhe tells the loss
Of the great fight when the Croppies met the Caithness
Legion: the date, 1798, cut in brass,

The man driving the forklift truck said: Keep on
Straight up the road and you'll see the monument
And turn to your right. But when I had gone

Up the long hill to the cross of Kilnagros,
I saw only the spruces that had grown
Darkening green on either side of the stone.

After a mile I turned back and drove west, blinded
By dancing flaws in the light, as I passed
Under the planted trees, like dashed foam

Or the dashes of yellow and white on an old headstone.
Yet in that darkening light I saw the place,
Turned left and followed the falling road

For the graveyard. I searched for my great
Grandfather's name, Charles Cullinane, but I found
Only one Daniel, 1843, one headstone,

And in Kilmalooda I found Timothy's name
On a headstone in the long grass almost lost,
And Jeremiah's, and I found the name *Bence-Jones*,

1971, cut by Séamus Murphy who made my father's stone
In 1970, in the Botanics, and below that another name
In a different hand, Ken Thompson's, I recognized:

Ken Thompson carves the figure 9
In a different style, as in the stone he made
For my mother and her second husband in their Offaly grave.

I left the Bence-Joneses in the long grass
And drove back to the cross
And downhill again past the secret monument

To the dead of the great battle of Kilnagros
*Where the spruces whistle to each other and the carved stone
    is lost.*

Grace Nichols

TEST MATCH HIGH MASS

(at Bourda Green, Georgetown, Guyana)

If Jesus was pressed into playing
a game, I'm sure it would be cricket
and he – the wicket-keeper
bearing open-palmed witness
behind the trinity of stumps.

Watching his white-clad disciples
work the green fields –
tracking the errant red soul
of a ball – arcing gloriously
across the turf of uncertainty.

Watching his flocks, especially
those in the trees (reminding him
of Zachias in his sycamore).
Now see them they flapping wings
at every six and four.

Meanwhile the sun
casting benediction down
but the two umpires
like judgement-day vicars
casting fate with a lift of finger –

Dis is high mass. Dis is Bourda.
We, the heaving congregation,
with a Job-like patience,
wonder what miracles will spin
to feed a hungry multitude?

Adam O'Riordan

Scar Tissue

When my hand finds your arm in the dark,
more often than not it's that glossy cicatrice
where one drunk winter you fell asleep
against the dull heat of a cast-iron radiator.
My fingers map the known world of its contour:
your lonely archipelago. The keloid scar grows
and grows until it will not let either of us go.
Greek *eschara*, your 'place of fire', defines you:
that intimacy with the impulses that drew
you to burn for a love you could not name,
and walking home in the drizzling rain
the man, inarticulate with rage, who flicks
a flame towards the shadow of the Cutty Sark.

Eleanor Rees

Spillage

Rain-glossed wood,
a lizard's back. Scales

shiny touched by rain –
the whole of the day in each drop.

Under, a fox settles in an oval
of dark dust. Soil

heavens enclose his matted fur
in dryness –

head tucked on paws,
streaked with a film of mud.

On the roof of the earth,
inside is sheltered from wetness

and my home beyond woodland:
room, leather, varnished oak.

Inside here I find blood, marrow,
purple-ordered brain, openings of lungs.

How to move through these?
How to find myself there?

To curl under a weight of self
and sleep at the centre and be sure.

David Sergeant

Sweetheart, they lined the street: the whites, browns, blacks,
The browns and blacks, the whites, the rich and poor,
Christian, Muslim, whatever, they stood together,
And fireworks were what they stood there for.

Each face upturned, each group outside its house.
I went by everyone – well, you know me –
And went unseen, they did not watch each other,
But parents knelt by children so they'd see

Each blast above the park, each rain of fire,
They pointed each one down, watched each one burn…
You know these people, see them every day,
Familiars from our makeshift segregation,

But separate – not like this, where each is joined
But separate, like the contents of a census,
Or sacks laid round to anchor the balloon
As it swells into the sky and starts to rise

And goes into the ropes and ropes them tight,
The sky itself flung off, replaced by burning…
Later I went into the park – a crowd – a fire
A pile of crates as massive as a building

But weeping off itself in walls of flame
That were not walls, but flashed rehearsals,
An image of itself that came again,
And again, and again, as if it might, was hopeful

That one day it would come right. I left
Before it could crumble into slush.

Its heat was still on my face when I came here,
Scared, too late, to give you this, too late,

My love, my not-enough, perhaps-enough.

John Stammers

MR PUNCH IN SOHO

You would recognise that hook nose anywhere,
his hump and paunch, the shiny pink erection of his chin.
Withered, crossed legs on the barstool
dangle like transplants from a much smaller body.
He could have found his ideal slot in the Gestapo,
been a dab hand with a blinding iron.
And the scold's bridle would have been right up his Strasse.
He has, they say, killed seven police:
old-time rozzers on the beat
more deserving of a saucy come-on from the street girls
than the last rites down a back alley.
And two wives. Poor old Mrs Punch finally copped it
one night after he'd done a few dozen barley wines
and as many double gins. She fought fiercely
against an *assailant or assailants unknown*
the Pall Mall Gazette reported. Never caught.
Never charged. And pretty little Mrs Punch
number two won't be taking a bath
in those bubbles again. That's the way to do it!
Just picture him afterwards, cock in hand
like an old chimp with a hard, green-tipped banana.
And the baby, where's the baby?
It's something to make the Devil into the good guy:
how children cry out for him
to drag Punch down to hell for eternal punishment.
But he'd throttle Lucifer when his back was turned
and be back on that stool for closing time.
Or maybe that's where he's been all these years
of grown-up sleep, peaceful and free of nightmare.
It's what you can't see in the stare of his wooden yellow eye.
Don't look, there's his stick, the awful stick!

Mary Turley McGrath

TRANSITIONS

The lake became an estuary overnight;
besieged by hammering rain,
flattened, subdued to shallows
of dark foil-strips between trees.
The drooping hazels and alders offered
no consolation; the sky was falling,
impaling itself on tips of forest pines;
it descended to enwrap the lake.

The heron had left for the lawn,
neck pushed forward in disdain;
the deluge had soaked him
to an alabaster shape. Then, near
the copper-beech, he took flight
across the grass and was gone.

Derek Walcott

White Egrets

I

Cautious of time's light and how often it will allow
the morning shadows to lengthen across the lawn
the stalking egrets to wriggle their beaks and swallow
when you, not they, or you and they, are gone;
for clattering parrots to launch their fleet at sunrise
for April to ignite the African violet
in the drumming world that dampens your tired eyes
behind two clouding lenses, sunrise, sunset,
the quiet ravages of diabetes.
Accept it all with level sentences
with sculpted settlement that sets each stanza,
learn how the bright lawn puts up no defences
against the egret's stabbing questions and the night's answer.

II

The elegance of those white, orange-billed egrets,
each like a stalking ewer, the thick olive trees,
cedars consoling a stream that roars torrentially
in the wet season; into that peace
beyond desires and beyond regrets,
at which I may arrive eventually,
whose palms droop in the sun like palanquins
with tigerish shadows under them. They shall
be there after my shadow passes with all its sins
into a green thicket of oblivion,
with the rising and setting of a hundred suns
over Santa Cruz Valley when I loved in vain.

III

I watch the huge trees tossing at the edge of the lawn
like a heaving sea without crests, the bamboos plunge
their necks like roped horses as yellow leaves, torn
from the whipping branches, turn to an avalanche;
all this before the rain scarily pours from the burst,
sodden canvas of the sky like a hopeless sail,
gusting in sheets and hazing the hills completely
as if the whole valley were a hull outriding the gale
and the woods were not trees but waves of a running sea.
When light cracks and thunder groans as if cursed
and you are safe in a dark house deep in Santa
Cruz, with the lights out, the current suddenly gone,
you think: "Who'll house the shivering hawk, and the
impeccable egret and the cloud-coloured heron,
and the parrots who panic at the false fire of dawn?"

IV

These birds keep modelling for Audubon,
the Snowy Egret or White Heron in a book
that, in my youth, would open like a lawn
in emerald Santa Cruz, knowing how well they look,
strutting perfection. They speckle the islands
on river-bank, in mangrove marsh or cattle pasture,
gliding over ponds, then balancing on the ridge
of a silken heifer, or fleeing disaster
in hurricane weather, and picking ticks
with their electric stab as if it were sheer privilege
to study them in their mythical conceit
that they have beat across the sea from Egypt
with the pharaonic ibis, its orange beak and feet
profiled in quiet to adorn a crypt,
then launch themselves with wings that, beating faster,
are certain as a seraph's when they beat.

V

The perpetual ideal is astonishment.
The cool green lawn, the quiet trees, the forest
on the hill there, then, the white gasp of an egret sent
sailing into the frame then teetering to rest
with its gawky stride, erect, an egret-emblem!
Another thought surprises: a hawk on the wrist
of a branch, soundlessly, like a falcon,
shoots into heaven, circling above praise or blame,
with the same high indifference as yours,
now dropping to tear a field mouse with its claws.
The page of the lawn and this open page are the same,
an egret astonishes the page, the high hawk caws
over a dead thing, a love that was pure punishment.

VI

I hadn't seen them for half of the Christmas week,
the egrets, and no one told me why they had gone,
but they are back with the rain now, orange beak,
pink shanks and stabbing head, back on the lawn
where they used to be in the clear, limitless rain
of the Santa Cruz Valley, which, when it rains, falls
steadily against the cedars till it mists the plain.
The egrets are the colour of waterfalls,
and of clouds. Some friends, the few I have left,
are dying, but the egrets stalk through the rain
as if nothing mortal can affect them, or they lift
like abrupt angels, sail, then settle again.
Sometimes the hills themselves disappear
like friends, slowly, but I am happier
that they have come back now, like memory, like prayer.

VII

With the leisure of a leaf falling in the forest,
pale yellow spinning against green – my ending.
Soon it will be the dry season, the hills will rust,
the egrets dip their necks undulant, bending,
stabbing at worms and grubs after the rain,
sometimes erect as bowling pins, they stand
as strips of cotton-wool peel from the mountain,
then when they move, gawkily, they move this hand
with their feet's splayed fingers, their darting necks.
We share one instinct, that ravenous feeding
my pen's beak, plucking up wriggling insects
like nouns and gulping them, the nib reading
as it writes, shaking off angrily what its beak rejects,
selection is what the egrets teach
on the wide open lawn, heads nodding as they read
in purposeful silence, a language beyond speech.

VIII

We were by the pool of a friend's house in St. Croix
and Joseph and I were talking; he stopped the talk,
on this visit I had hoped that he would enjoy
to point out, with a gasp, not still or stalking
but fixed in the great fruit tree, a sight that shook him
"like something out of Bosch," he said. The huge bird was
suddenly there, perhaps the same one that took him,
a sepulchral egret or heron; the unutterable word was
always with us, like Eumaeus, a third companion
and what got him, who loved snow, what brought it on
was that the bird was such a spectral white.
Now when at noon or evening on the lawn
the egrets soar together in noiseless flight
or tack, like a regatta, the sea-green grass,
they are seraphic souls, as Joseph was.

C K Williams

FROG

Naturally Annie Dillard
knew when she inserts at the outset
of a book a water beetle's
devouring a frog
that the description would shock –

the bug injects enzymes
that dissolve the frog's "organs
and bones...all but the skin..."
and sucks the poor
liquefied creature out of itself –

but I doubt if she'd have guessed
how often her awful anecdote
could come back, at least
to someone like me, always
with revulsion and terror.

Last night I woke in the dark
with *"It burns!"* in my mind:
the voice was mine, the tone
a child's anguished cry
to a parent, the image the frog,

and the thought – is that the word?
I hardly knew where I was
that this was worse
than nightmare, to regress
awake from the realm of reason.

Dillard is erudite, tender
and wise, and she can be funny –
remember her imagining

literally replicating a tree? –
and she understands

where our animal nature
ends and our human begins,
but this, slayer and slain,
cruelty and, she says it herself,
"the waste of pain…"

When I look down in
the murk of the brook
here, I see only chains
of bubbles rising
sporadically from the slime.

Are there beings there, too,
living their own fear-driven
dream? Is the mud itself
trying to breathe?
If so, must it hurt?

Publisher acknowledgements

Fleur Adcock · FAST FORWARD · *Dragon Talk* · Bloodaxe Books

Simon Armitage · POODLES · *Seeing Stars* · Faber and Faber

Simon Armitage · THE LIVES OF THE POETS · Poetry News

Kate Bingham · ON HIGHGATE HILL · *Times Literary Supplement*

Alison Brackenbury · THE JOBBING WELDER · Poetry Wales

Christian Campbell · VERTIGO · LIGHTSKINNED ID · *Running the Dusk* · Peepal Tree Press

Siobhán Campbell · WHEN I ASKED MY DAD ABOUT WARRENPOINT · *Cross-Talk* · Seren

Julia Copus · AN EASY PASSAGE · Magma

Kwame Dawes · REGENERATION · *Back of Mount Peace* · Peepal Tree Press

Tom Duddy · THE TOUCH · Smiths Knoll

Carol Ann Duffy · A RARE BEE · *Times Literary Supplement*

Elaine Feinstein · CHRISTMAS DAY IN WILLESDEN GREEN · *Cities* · Carcanet

Alistair Findlay · DANCING WITH BIG EUNICE · *Dancing with Big Eunice* · Luath Press

John Fuller · THREE TIMES · *Pebble & I* · Chatto & Windus

Lydia Fulleylove · NIGHT DRIVE · Bridport Prize

Damian Furniss · THE DUCHESS OF KALIGHAT · *Chocolate Che* · Shearsman Books

Rebecca Goss · MRS QUIGLEY AND I · *The Anatomy of Structures* · Flambard Press

Philip Gross · THE PRESENCE · *The Water Table* · Bloodaxe Books

David Harsent · BLOOD · Poetry Review

Seamus Heaney · 'HAD I NOT BEEN AWAKE' · MIRACLE · *Human Chain* · Faber and Faber

Rachael Hegarty · COCKLE PICKER · Crannog

Tony Hoagland · IN PRAISE OF THEIR DIVORCE · *Unincorporated Persons in the Late Honda Dynasty* · Bloodaxe Books

Anthony Howell · STRETCH · *The Ogre's Wife* · Anvil Press

Ishion Hutchinson · REQUIEM FOR AUNT MAY · *Far District Poems* · Peepal Tree

Chris Jones · SENTENCES · Staple